RIGHTLY DIVIDED

A beginner's guide to bible study

J. Michael Lester

Cover Design: Levi D. Jones
levidjones.com

DEDICATION

I love my family. In the words of the Apostle John, I have
no greater joy than to hear that my children walk in truth.
This book is dedicated to them to help them continue in
that path of truth. Thank you to my wonderful wife and
great daughters whose questions and comments have
helped me to offer a book on Bible study that is reachable
for those who need "the bottom shelf."

CONTENTS

INTRODUCTION

Have you ever opened your Bible and just stared at it? You've made this time for Bible study – it's on your calendar. You have set your morning appointment with God and your Bible. Why? Simply stated – you know it will help you. Yet, you just sit and stare, feeling more lost with each fleeting moment. Perhaps you are thinking that 1 Chronicles wasn't the best place to start. Leviticus wasn't helping much either. Then you thought, "Aha, I'll go to the New Testament." But Revelation was giving you nightmares!

You know you should do more than simply read the Bible. You've been told that you are to "study to show yourself approved…" And, you really want to do this! Yet, you do not know either where to start in the Bible or even how to begin the whole process of Bible study. It's a frustrating feeling. Somehow, you think your Bible is just sitting there mocking you – daring you to make sense of this ancient Book! Take courage – you are not alone!

As a singles' pastor, I have had the privilege of personally mentoring and discipling new believers for over twenty years. Often, these people cannot even find the book of Ephesians – much less know that it is a book in the

Bible. I grew up in the Bible Belt in the heart of the South. Almost everyone there claimed to be a Christian and, generally speaking, had some understanding of the Bible. That is no longer true today. Many people are coming to this discussion biblically illiterate. This book begins with that assumption and is truly a beginner's guide to understanding how to study the Bible.

For today's disciples, who are just beginning to study the Bible, staring at a table of contents with sixty-six books can feel a bit overwhelming – perhaps, even intimidating. Do you start with Leviticus? (No!) Do you start with a book study? Do you study a topic? If so, which topic do you study? Do you just cherry pick references until you convince yourself the Bible agrees with your plan? (No!)

If these types of questions describe you, then rest assured that this book is written with you in mind. In the next few chapters, I will walk you through a simple three-step process to help you trade the milk for the meat of the Word. As the subtitle suggests, we are getting down to the basic guidelines for understanding your Bible. You really can study the Bible on your own and actually enjoy it! I'm not suggesting that Bible study is easy; but I am saying that you can do this!

As a Bible college instructor, I have had the privilege to teach both basic and advanced hermeneutics (hermeneutics is the art and science of interpreting the Bible) for over two decades. What is taught in this book has been hammered out in the classroom. It really works! One of the joys I have in being a teacher is watching a student have one of those "aha!" moments when the light comes on and the process clicks. In this book, you get the same basic concepts that I have shared with college students – at a substantial discount! You, too, can have your "aha!" moment as you begin to practice the concepts laid out before you.

I can imagine you shaking your head in disbelief. Perhaps you resist, saying, "That just sounds too easy!" or "I'm not Bible college material!" Not only has this material been taught in the Bible college setting, it has also been taught in the Sunday school classroom with ordinary every-day believers who are just trying to live for Jesus. And, while the concept is easy, don't be fooled into thinking that there is no work involved!

Across America, and really throughout the entire world, Bible teachers and preachers stand behind lecterns and deliver the truths of God's Word that they have discovered utilizing this same three-step process. You can do this too. Imagine standing in front of your family and confidently teaching them the Bible. Think about having the skill-set needed to answer the skeptic at work who always asks you questions, but you are not sure on how to find the answer. Ponder the thought of being able to sit down and tackle a tough topic and then say authoritatively, "This is what the Bible says about this subject." Your co-worker wants to know your thought about moving in with his girlfriend – the Bible has an answer to that. The neighbor next-door wants to know if the Bible speaks to when life begins – it does! Having answers to people's questions is a great way to open doors for telling people about Christ. That's what this book will help you accomplish.

I'm the kind of teacher who likes to stay in touch with students. Often I'll ask them, "What was the most helpful class you took?" Sometimes, it is a question like, "What is one class you wish you had taken or wish we had offered?" One former student who is now a pastor said his most helpful course in all of college was his hermeneutics class. This testimony has been repeated by both men and women who have had their "aha" moment and the intimidation factor of Bible study removed. The reason for writing this book is to increase those "aha" moments to far beyond the college classroom. People in churches today want to know how to get into the Word – they are simply waiting for a guide. I'm not a perfect guide – but together we can at least move from the "I really need to do this" to "I'm actually doing this!"

If you will take these three steps to heart and commit to practicing what is taught, you will be able to get much more out of your Bible study. These three steps are to be taken in order – you will not find a shortcut here! However, you will discover that Bible teachers do not have a secret knowledge that is inaccessible to the rest of the congregation. Sure, some people are gifted teachers – yet, Bible study is a skill set that any one can master. The great Bible teachers simply have diligence to faithfully utilize a method that helps them do more than simply read the Bible, check off a daily reading schedule, and then forget what they have read. These people study, reflect, apply, and teach to others. You can do the same.

Bible study is still work. Two thousand years ago, the veteran apostle Paul told his young protégé, Timothy, to study the Scriptures. In this command found in 2 Timothy 2:15, Paul referenced a "workman" who would rightly divide the word of truth in this process. He made no lofty promises – he told Timothy that work was involved. Yet, the destination – the ability to rightly divide Scriptures for yourself – is worth the work. So, go ahead and make the commitment to go from milk to meat. Remember that ultimately the workman who rightly divides the word of truth has God's approval on his life.

Don't be content to be spoon-fed by another pastor or Bible teacher. Learn to dig in for yourself and find those hidden treasures in God's Word. The tone of this book is very conversational. In writing this book, I have pictured myself sitting across a coffee table, telling you face-to-face how to get more out of Bible study. This is not a dry, academic textbook. I definitely don't want Bible study to be boring! With that said, now it's time for you to learn this process. What are you waiting for?!

1

GET READY!

Before you simply open your Bible and start studying, there are some basic instructions you need. If you are the type of person who gets the car already going down the street before punching the address in the GPS, I identify with you! Yet, when it comes to Bible study, let's keep the car parked for a moment and figure out where we need to go first!

In this chapter, you will learn how to prepare yourself to receive the most out of Bible study. Additionally, you will learn the process of how to establish Bible study as a habit, a routine rather than simply something you do every once in a blue moon! Deep down, you already know that if you can establish the habit of Bible study and learn the tools to make the process effective, you will be a much stronger Christian.

One summer, as I was working my way through Bible college. I had a job as an electrician. I was a total newbie and can still remember being sent out to the truck to get the "wire stretchers." (There is no such thing…my co-workers had a great time laughing at me after I went looking for them three different times in the truck!) Over time, I learned the basics, and eventually wired my own personal house. How did I get to that point? Simple: On day one, my boss took me to the supply house and bought me a tool belt, some hand tools, wire nuts, and much more. Then he worked with me one-on-one and showed me how to do it. He prepared me – then he taught me. That's what I want to do in this book for you. So, how do we prepare?

Understand what the terms mean…

I promise to keep this book simple. It is written with beginners in mind. However, you may have read other books or heard terms that sound too much like "preacher-talk." In case those words come up, it's good to have a simple, working definition for each of them. Here are the most common:

1. Hermeneutics

This term is the technical word that describes the process of interpreting the Bible. Hermeneutics is both an art and a science. It is a science because there are some simple rules that always guide the process. It is also an art in that the more you participate in the process, the better you become at it. I'm not sure that practice makes perfect – but I definitely believe that practice makes progress.

Hermes was the Greek messenger god, sent to bear witness for Zeus. In Acts 14, Paul and Barnabas are thought to be the gods sent to man. Because Paul does the speaking, they assume that he is *Hermes* (Roman god, Mercury) and that Barnabas is *Zeus* (Roman god, Jupiter). Luke uses a form of this name in Luke 24:27, when Jesus *expounded* or explained everything to them. This is the root word from which hermeneutics originates.

2. Exegesis

This technical term (and its related words, *exegete* and *exegetical*) describes the emphasis of the process. The prefix *ex-* indicates that someone is drawing the meaning <u>out of</u> the text. In this process, the Bible student is endeavoring to understand the writer's intent and to comprehend how the original audience would have understood him.

You may never use this word, or the next one, in a sentence. But at the very least, I hope you will learn that Bible study is pulling the meaning *out of the text* rather than reading the meaning *into the text*.

3. Eisegesis

This word is just the opposite of exegesis. Whereas exegesis deals with pulling the meaning out of the text, eisegesis is when the interpreter reads his meaning *into* the text. His interpretation is clouded by his own biases, his own presuppositions, and his own theology. Rather than seeing what the text actually says, this process is often used to attempt to prove one's own theology.

Here's a classic example. John 3:16 says, "For God so loved *the world*..." Yet, you can find commentaries that say just the opposite. "It's obvious that God does not love *everyone*; He only loves those whom He has promised to save." How could they get that from the text? They didn't! They imported that meaning from their theology to the text – and that's dangerously wrong.

As an aside, every Bible reader should be transparent enough to recognize he comes to the Bible with some biases, some presuppositions, and some strongly held beliefs that he assumes / hopes / believes the Bible teaches. Many times, the Bible will confirm those beliefs. However, at times it may insist that we change our beliefs to conform to the Bible. The Bible does not conform to us; we conform to it!

4. Context

I am not sure who first said it, but it has been repeated often: "A text without a context is only a pretext." What does that mean? In Bible study, we are not simply doing "word studies" or asking, "What does this verse mean?" We are not even asking, "What does this verse mean to me?" A verse is not a stand-alone component meant to be understood in isolation. Rather, the verse is part of a paragraph, which is part of a chapter, which is part of a book. This is the *context* in which the verse is found.

Did you know that the Bible actually says, "There is no God…" In fact, you can read this exact phrase twice in Psalm 14:1 and Psalm 53:1. Yet, what I have just written is *completely out of context*! The full phrase is "The fool hath said, There is no God." If someone doesn't care about context, he can make the Bible teach just about any thing he wants! Context is very important in understanding the Bible's message. Remember, the passage cannot mean what it never meant!

Consider this promise: [Jehovah speaking] "I will make of thee a great nation…" Be careful before you claim that "promise." In the context, God is speaking *to Abraham* (Genesis 12).

5. Historical-grammatical approach

This term has a few other synonyms that explain the process. Some writers will talk about the *literal* approach. "We interpret the Bible literally." Others balk at that term because they feel as though it doesn't allow for parts of the Bible that are figurative. A term I use often is the *normal* approach. Years ago, a man named Cooper said, "If

the plain sense makes common sense, seek no other
sense for that would be nonsense." What he meant
was that common sense could help a reader know
when something was figurative. When Jesus says,
"I am the true vine…" common sense helps us
realize that He is not a literal vine!

So, this historical-grammatical process has
two parts: a historical context and a grammatical
context. The historical context helps us understand
the audience. We are asking, "How would they have
understood this letter or book?" The grammatical
context pays attention to the sentence structure,
asking if there is a command, a question, a
statement, etc.

Start with the end in mind…

Solomon, the wisest man that ever lived, taught that
the end of a thing was better than the beginning
(Ecclesiastes 7:8). He also stated that the accomplished
desire was sweet to the soul (Proverbs 13:19). So, before
we even open the Bible, I need to ask you a question, "Why
are you doing this? What do you hope to learn from this
process?" These two questions deal with your goal and
your motives – both of which are important.

Jesus told a religious group in John 5:39 to "search
the Scriptures." Then He stated that those Scriptures (the
Old Testament was all this group had) testified of Jesus and
that in these Scriptures they would find life. Therefore, one

of the goals of Bible study (as well as a motive) is to know God better. The Bible is His love letter to us – we read it to know *about* Him and to know Him.

There are lesser motives that bring some people to Bible study. Some people simply want to prove their friends wrong about a doctrine. Others even come to prove the Bible wrong. Because we believe context is the key, we are not pulling verses here and there to simply prove a point. Rather, we are looking at the big picture and asking, "What can I learn about God here?"

Practical pointers...

Forgive me if this sounds too basic. But before you even open the Bible, you should pray and ask the Author (the Holy Spirit) to help you understand what He has written. You are not interpreting my letters! You are working to understand His. While there is the art and science of hermeneutics, there is also the Spirit's role in illumination. Let's not ignore Him in this process.

Do you journal or keep a diary? Some do; some don't. Yet, I would encourage you to journal your thoughts for Bible study as you get started. Perhaps you will do this electronically with something like Evernote. Perhaps you will have an actual physical journal. Whichever route you choose, the purpose is so that you can keep track of what you are learning as well as have a place to write down what you still want to study later.

There is something to be said about consistency as well. So determine now – when will you study your Bible? Where will you study your Bible? Are you a morning person? Are you a night owl? Should you sit at the kitchen table with a cup of coffee? How about that favorite chair in the family room? Where can you have some quiet, undistracted time to start working through the Bible? Whatever you decide on these questions, make a commitment to yourself to develop this discipline – and tell someone about it!

Yes, actually tell someone you trust that you will be studying the Bible each morning at 5:30 with coffee in your favorite chair in the family room. Why? Our human nature needs the accountability to help us develop the habit. If no one knows of our new resolution, no one will know when we miss this appointment either. In our Western culture, we have become highly individualistic. Yet, one look at the early church and one observes it was highly community-oriented. Those early believers understood that the church was a body, a team that worked together rather than alone. So, get past your individualistic tendencies and live in the community. Tell a friend about your decision and ask that person to periodically check in and see how it's going. It will help you and it might just encourage someone else to get involved in Bible study as well. Who will that person be? Decide today and make that call.

Trusted Tools

Obviously you will need a Bible to get this process started! I'm often asked, "There are so many different choices – I'm overwhelmed. Can you just recommend a Bible for me?" Study Bibles are not a one-size-fits-all. However, I will at least state that there were two study Bibles I used in the beginning (and a third one I'll mention with a caveat!).

I believe the first Bible I ever personally bought was when I was about 11 or 12 years old. I saved and purchased a Bible called "The Open Bible." Later I bought two more of these types and had an additional one given to me. At the front of this Bible was an encyclopedic index of topics listed alphabetically. Each topic had multiple verses listed. It was a great place to begin a topical Bible study. This Bible also had helpful articles inserted throughout the text as well as a section that would help with understanding some of the basic cultures and customs of the Bible land. I also enjoyed the fact that it would take those ancient sounding monetary terms and provide a note of how much that would be worth in today's dollars. This was a really helpful Bible and I would recommend it as a great place to start. Online, this Bible starts at about $60.

I also used a Thompson's Chain Reference Bible. To be honest, I didn't use it as much as the Open Bible, but this Bible was a great aid in helping me learn how to put passages together. One of the principles of interpretation you'll learn in chapter three is that we use the Bible to interpret the Bible. Bibles with chain references make this task easier. This Bible costs about the same.

The third Bible I used in the early days was the famous Scofield Reference Bible. I enjoyed its chain references as well as the study notes it provided. Scofield was influential in helping bring some end-times positions back to a majority. Here's the caveat: Scofield's notes are not inspired! As a kid, I remember going to camp meetings in the South and hearing preachers preach from the notes (rather than the text). The notes are helpful, but they can't replace what God has given us.

You may be thinking, "All I have is my $5 gift Bible." That's great for reading…but you want more! You want to understand the text. While you can study a Bible which has no notes, I would not recommend it. That's like trying to build a house armed only with a hammer. You might eventually get the job done, but you will certainly take the long way (and the wrong way) to do it. Bible study is easier when we have the right tools.

Let me mention a few more tools that would be helpful for you to put in your toolbox. Some of these tools can be found online for free. At a very minimum, besides a good study Bible, here are the tools I suggest you get:

1. Strong's Concordance

When I surrendered my life to be a teacher and preacher of the Word of God, one of my uncles purchased this book for me and had my name engraved upon it. The Strong's Concordance takes every word used in the English Bible and shows you what Hebrew (if from the Old Testament) or Greek (if from the New Testament) word from which it is translated.

This concordance will help you identify every place this word is found so you can see it in other contexts. Additionally, it provides the other English words our translators used to convey the original word's meaning. In this sense, you are able to get a fuller picture of how this word, with all of its nuances, is used in the Bible.

FINANCIAL INVESTMENT: $0. Because this tool can be accessed online, all you need is a connection. Here is a site you should bookmark for future reference.
http://www.biblestudytools.com/concordances/.

This tool is also bundled with some inexpensive Bible software such as PowerBible or Olive Tree.

2. Nave's or Torrey's Topical Bible

These resources are just what they sound like. You want to study a topic – but how do you even get started? These two resources are what you use to help jumpstart that study. Simply look up the topic, then begin reading the references provided.

FINANCIAL INVESTMENT: $0.
Torrey's Topical Textbook is also available online
for free. Book mark this site for future reference:
http://www.biblestudytools.com/concordances/torre
ys-topical-textbook/.

3. Webster's 1828 Dictionary

Sometimes the Bible uses theological terms
that are not as familiar to today's English speakers.
Words such as *propitiation* can stop a new Bible
student in his tracks. The 1828 Webster's edition
(found online) is unique in that it has helped to
define words in the English language. In fact, it
often used Bible verses in its sample sentences. The
Christian foundation behind the defining of the
English words helps this to become a trusted
resource you can reference.

FINANCIAL INVESTMENT: $0. Once
again, here is a tool that is available for free online.
Bookmark this site:
http://webstersdictionary1828.com.

4. Bible Dictionary

There are a few different Bible dictionaries
available today. Basically, each option has the same
goal in mind: to define biblical concepts and words.

FINANCIAL INVESTMENT: $0. This is
another tool you do not need to purchase because

many sites have these available for free online. Bookmark this site for your use: http://www.biblestudytools.com/dictionaries/ for some free options.

5. A One-Volume Commentary such as Graham Scroggie (*The Unfolding Drama of Redemption*) or J. Sidlow Baxter's *Explore the Book.*

     I recommend a good one-volume commentary as a ready reference when you come to a passage that may be difficult. Scroggie's book helps to locate each book within the framework of God's plan of redemption. Remember that Jesus said that the Old Testament spoke about Him? Scroggie helps the reader to see how each book does that.

     FINANCIAL INVESTMENT: $15. For a new copy, this would be more expensive. However, sometimes a previous edition can be found for about $15 on Amazon.

     Baxter's book is like a complete survey course of both Old and New Testaments. This book is a little pricier and may not be part of your Bible study budget. But if you can get it, it is highly recommended.

     FINANCIAL INVESTMENT: $60. This is probably the most expensive book I will mention.

You can do without it. But once the process becomes more natural to you, you may think about adding this book later. As of publishing, this book was about $60 on Amazon.

6. Computer Software

I am not a representative of any software company or publisher. I am not working on commission here! However, if we were sitting across from each other at a table, many of you would ask me, "What do you use?"

I started out with PowerBible CD. It was probably about a $10 investment or less. It works for PC / Windows computers. It has 22 Bible translations, 10 Bible dictionaries, 10 topical references, 20 commentaries, and Strong's Concordance. It's a good beginner tool – but not helpful for Mac / Apple users.

Many years ago, I was introduced to Libronix / Logos 3 (yes, many years ago!). Today, it is simply known as Logos and I have a little over 7,000 resources in my current package. It is not for the faint of heart and requires a substantial investment. What I will share with you in this book is enough to get started. However, once you have mastered the technique, this might be a software worth looking at. When you come to that cross road, contact me – I'll give you my honest assessment!

In this chapter, we have covered the basics to getting ready. We have tried to point out the "why" for Bible study (to know God better). We have covered the importance of consistency (when, where, and who will you tell). We have even received some trusted resources to help get this process started. You should now be ready to begin the journey of Bible interpretation.

In the next chapter, you will learn the first of three steps for this process. However, before you move to the next chapter, do something about this chapter! Check off the action items below:

- ☐ I have an accountability partner.
- ☐ I have a study Bible.
- ☐ I have determined my "when" and "where" to study the Bible.
- ☐ I have clarity on why I am studying the Bible.
- ☐ I have bookmarked the online Bible study tools for easy reference.

2

WHY COULDN'T I SEE THAT?

Have you ever sat in utter amazement at a Bible lesson you were hearing at a church service (or at a time when the Bible was being taught)? Have you ever thought to yourself, "I've never seen that before…" Or, perhaps you have even phrased this as a question, "How did that teacher get all of that from those verses?" If so, you are not alone! Sometimes, coming home from church after a powerful sermon, a similar comment has been made by me, my wife, or one of the kids.

When I was a new Christian, I thought that these teachers simply had a secret insight into Scripture that I could never have. Perhaps you have thought the same – there's "those guys who understand the Bible" and then, there's the rest of us. Yet, the reality is that you can find these same truths using the three-step process in this book.

You will actually be able to sit down with a co-worker or family member and tell them the background for the book of John. You will be able to not only know John 3:16 is a familiar verse, you will be able to understand what is happening in John 3 that makes verse 16 so important. This brings us to…

Step 1: Observation

Rather than define this step, I want to involve you.

Could you do me a favor? Go to this site: https://www.houzz.com/photos/36935767/April-Fool-Artwork-traditional-prints-and-posters and look at a picture by Norman Rockwell. It was an April Fool's Day cover for the Saturday Evening Post in 1943. At first glance, it is a picture of an elderly couple playing checkers in front of their fireplace. Yet, I need you to get past the first glance…stare a little longer. Are there some things "not quite right?" How many problems can you find?

Rockwell stated that there were 45 errors in this picture. At first glance, you do not notice these things. Yet, the more you observe, the more you see. Developing this skill is the first step for Bible study. Take a quick look at this as well:

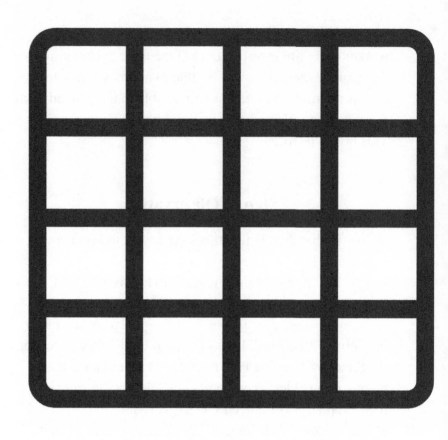

How many squares do you see? Take a *really* good look. (Hint: You should see more than 16!)

Frankly, I am not going to give you the answer – I'll let you come back to this picture a few times. But as you begin to "observe" the details, you notice that there is one big square that surrounds the sixteen little ones. Then, you can see all of the 2x2 squares, as well as the 3x3 squares that are here. And that's just counting the white spaces –

what about the small squares that are formed by the intersections of the black grid lines?!

You may be thinking what does staring at a bunch of squares or a 70+ year-old painting have to do with Bible study? The answer is, "Everything!" Both of these illustrations graphically represent the principle behind step one – learning to observe the text.

When I told you that Rockwell's painting had errors in it, you began to look a little harder. Maybe you saw the deer under the man's chair (it's not a dog). Maybe you saw the fish coming down the stairwell. Maybe, you even noticed that a stairwell directly behind the fireplace would be a code violation! When I told you there was more than 16 squares and even pointed out a few places to look, you began to "see it." What I want to do in this chapter is show you what to look for as you observe the Bible text.

What is the context?
We defined *context* in the "Getting Ready" chapter. Again I use the often repeated phrase, "A text without a context is only a pretext!" If a person cares little about context, he can make the Bible teach just about anything (let me say, "incorrectly teach" just about anything!)

It's a ridiculous story, but it illustrates this point. A fellow was needing some guidance in his life and knew that the Word of God was a "lamp to his feet" and a "light to his path." Not knowing where to start, he simply opened his Bible and pointed to a verse at random.

And he cast down the pieces of silver in the temple, and departed, and went and hanged himself. Matthew 27:5

Certainly this could not be the will of God for him. So, he closed his Bible, took a deep breath, and tried again. This time he read,

Coming to Luke 10:37, his eyes found the last phrase, *Go and do thou likewise.*

Again, he was troubled. Could this really be God speaking to him? So, he closed the Bible and opened it again for the final time. This time he came to John 13:27 where he read,

That thou doest, do quickly.

He had read, "He went and hanged himself." This was followed by "Go and do thou likewise," and even by "Do quickly!" In this proverbial story, we find a man who needs to look at the context!

So, you know context is important. But how do you find it? We've all heard a preacher make a passage come alive by painting a picture of what is happening in the background. In his presence, you feel as though you are apart of the passage – living it. Personally, I find it helpful to know the historical context in a passage. Let's take a famous incident from the gospel of John. In chapter four, Jesus is in Samaria, talking with the "woman at the well." At first glance, this is just a story of Jesus being thirsty and asking the first person He sees for water. *This is looking at the story like it was in black and white!* What if we could see it in HD?

In setting this context, there are a few questions we should ask:
1. Is Samaria significant to understanding this text?
2. What mountain is she talking about? ("Our fathers worshipped in this mountain…")
3. What can we learn about the character of the woman?

Sometimes, in setting the historical context, we need some outside help. This is where we go to one of those one-volume commentaries or the Bible study tools found online. I recommend that you even open to the back of your study Bible and look at the maps to visualize where Samaria is located.

As you begin to look up Samaria in Bible dictionaries and encyclopedias, here is what you will find. Back in the Old Testament, Israel eventually divided into a Northern and Southern Kingdom after the death of Solomon. The Northern Kingdom, called Israel, was eventually carried away captive by the Assyrians. The Assyrians repopulated the land with natives from all over their conquered territories. The end result of this was that some of the Jewish people who had been left behind intermarried with some of these Gentile pagans. This mixed race came to be known as Samaritans.

The Jews from the Southern Kingdom, called Judah or Judea, were not happy with their Northern counterparts. They viewed these marriages as illegitimate and that the promised lineage of Abraham was being defiled. The hatred grew so strong that prejudices were even found among the 12 disciples (Luke 9:52-56 – James and John wanted to pray down fire to destroy a Samaritan village!). Eventually, most Jews would not even step foot in Samaria, choosing instead to cross over the Jordan River, and take the long way on their journeys into Galilee. So, the fact that Jesus "must needs go through Samaria" and that He actually talked with a Samaritan woman is significant.

Look at this Bible map to visualize what the average Jew did to get to Galilee. Leaving Jerusalem, they would cross the Jordan River, coming up through Perea and the Decapolis before crossing back over the Jordan River to get into Galilee. Such was the animosity the Jews had for the Samaritans that they did not even want to traverse through the Samaritan soil! So, when Jesus says, "Hey guys! I really need to go through Samaria for this trip…" – this was unexpected and perhaps a little uncomfortable for some in the group. They were all too ready to leave Jesus at the well alone and take cover.

Do you see how that little bit of background information brings some "color" to an otherwise black and white story?

As you continue to read about Samaria in your dictionaries, you find that this mountain adds some more details as well. About 100 years before Christ was born, a Jewish leader named John Hyrcanus gathered an army together. They marched into Samaria because a rival religion was developing as well as a rival temple. This temple had been built upon Mount Gerizim. John and his army destroyed this temple and many of the former pillars could be seen scattered on the mount as the woman spoke with Jesus. "Our fathers said we should worship here [at Mount Gerizim]. You Jewish people say we should worship there [in Jerusalem]." Jesus then helps this woman understand that it is not the location of the body that determines how one worships – instead we worship in spirit and truth.

These Samaritan ruins are still visible today.

Typically, women came in groups to get water. This provided some protection as well as a chance for fellowship. Yet this woman is coming at a different hour, alone. Why? As you read through the chapter, you learn that she has not been a very moral woman. She has been married five times and is currently living with a man who is not her husband. She is a scandal – the type of woman that simply invites gossip from other women.

We have learned a lot about the "context" of this passage before we have even begun to understand the passage's significance. Before moving on, let's review how we found this information:

1. **We asked questions**. What's the big deal about Samaria? What mountain is she talking about? What kind of woman was this?
2. **We found answers**. We went to our dictionaries, encyclopedias, and commentaries and learned from those who have already spent a lot of time in the passage.

What else should you do during this initial observation?

Read, and then read it again...

G. Campbell Morgan was a famous preacher from a different era. When he was preparing to teach a book, his practice was to read it through fifty times before he even began to start dissecting the various parts of the book. You may not have time to read through a book over and over again...however, you can read this chapter a few times.

As you read through a passage several times, you begin to understand the flow of it. You are helping to set the context of what is happening in your mind. You are also internalizing the Word of God. How many times have you read something, in the Bible or elsewhere, mindlessly?

Your mind goes to auto-pilot just waiting to get to the end of the chapter to check it off. Reading a passage again and again helps us to digest what is happening, even when our mind goes into auto mode.

Pay attention to the words

As you read through a passage several times, have your journal ready. Write down what you are observing. The habit of writing down is based upon the principle, "A short pencil is better than a long memory!" Additionally, when you involve more than just one of your senses, you remember it better. So, rather than simply "mentally observing" the text, take the time to write your observations as well. What should you be looking for?

1. Words that connect.

    I often hear people quote Hebrews 4:12 as, "The Word of God is quick and powerful..." It's not *quite* right. The verse actually begins with, "*For* the Word of God is quick and powerful..." The little word *for* is a connecting word. Before I simply quote this verse with no regard to its context, perhaps I should read verses 1-11 and see how this verse comes as a conclusion to what has been discussed.

    If you grew up going to teen camps or youth conferences, I am sure you have heard Romans 12:1 preached at least once. "I beseech you therefore, brethren, by the mercies of God, that ye present

your bodies a living sacrifice…" Usually a message
follows about surrender. However, if you are
observant, you may have noticed a connecting word
therefore.

Rule of thumb: Whenever you see the word
therefore, check to see why it's there for! If you
were really paying attention, you would also notice
that Paul is using plural pronouns here: "…that ye
present your bodies…" Western Christians can tend
to view the Scriptures through the lens of rugged
individualism; whereas, the first century church
understood the concept of community.

2. Words that are unfamiliar.
    How many times have you used the word
    propitiation in a sentence? Probably never! Yet, it's
    found in Romans 3 and 1 John 2. It's a rich,
    theological word – but it's a word that we should
    stop, pull out our dictionary, and define. This word,
    simply defined, is a satisfactory payment. Yet, even
    this begs the question – what or whom is being
    propitiated or satisfied?

    The longer definition of *propitiation* is the
    payment that satisfies the just demands of a holy
    God. As you can see, it is a great theological word –
    just unfamiliar to most people today.

3. Words that are repeated.

You see this often in the Psalms. Consider Psalm 136 where the last half of each verse is identical. Why? The psalmist, under the inspiration of the Holy Spirit, is stressing something to us. He does something similar in Psalm 119 in describing the Word of God. We need to be observant enough to pay attention. Paul also does this in 1 Corinthians 13 with the word *charity*.

Mark the paragraphs

Do you remember your high school English classes? I didn't ask if you remembered them fondly! One of the things you probably heard was that a paragraph has one main point. When I am working through Scripture, I find that if I can understand the paragraphs, it helps me to narrow in on the writer's meaning. I am now asking, "What is Paul's main point in this paragraph?" rather than looking at a group of verses independently.

How do we find the paragraphs? Here are our options:

1. Hope your study Bible uses this symbol: ¶
2. Mark your own paragraphs by following the writer's line of thought.
3. Utilize a Bible such as the Cambridge Paragraph Bible (my preference).

The paragraph Bible can be found online for free at https://biblia.com/books/av1873/Ge1.

Big Idea

Consider what you have already accomplished with the text up to this point. You have learned how to place a book or a chapter into its context. You have read through that chapter (or text) several times. You have looked at connecting words and tried to understand the connection.

Furthermore, you have looked at words that were unfamiliar and defined them. Additionally, you have looked at words that were repeated and understood their emphasis. You have marked out the paragraph that completes the section you are studying. You already know that in this paragraph, there is only one central idea. So, how do you find it?

Questions are a great resource in helping you investigate a paragraph's big idea. Try answering these questions about your text:

1. Is your paragraph part of a narrative, a story? If so, consider the characters and the plot.
2. What is the setting?
3. Perhaps just as importantly, what is the climax?

Let's put it to work. This process is especially valuable when working with parables. Remember the story of the Prodigal Son in Luke 15? As you begin to read in verse 1 (because you want to put it into a proper context!) you observe that this "story" is actually act 3 in an extended parable about lost things.

Act 1: A man has lost a sheep. He goes to search for it and finds it. Then he calls his friends to rejoice.

Act 2: A woman has lost a coin. She goes to search for it until she finds it. Then, she calls her friends to rejoice.

Act 3: A father has two sons. He "loses" one son (and has problems with the one who stayed home). He waits patiently until that son is found. Then, he calls all of his friends together and they rejoice.

In each act, there is rejoicing, and by implication of a cultural understanding – a meal. What prompts Jesus to tell this story? He was accused of *eating* with sinners. What is the climax of the parable? A father makes a lavish meal for a wayward son and invites the community to rejoice.

What if you are not working with a parable? Even then, questions are still a great tool to utilize. Are you reading an epistle with more instruction than story? If so, then consider asking these types of questions. What is the context in which it resides? What is the theme of the book in which the writer has written that portion? What point is the writer making? How could you reword this section to show that you have grasped its meaning?

Are you working through the poetical sections? How can you summarize or put into your own words what the writer is saying? How does this section teach you something about God? What was the historical context behind this psalm?

In this chapter, you have learned the first of three steps for productive Bible study. It is a skill that is developed the more you practice. In the next chapter you will jump into step two, *interpretation*. However, before you move to the next chapter, do something with this chapter! Check off the action items below:

- ☐ Read Romans 3 ten times.

- ☐ Read Romans 3:21-31 another ten times (this is a paragraph).

- ☐ Using information from your study Bible, dictionary, or commentary, write a brief paragraph setting the book of Romans into its historical context in your journal.

- ☐ Write down any unfamiliar, repeating, or connecting words in your journal.

- ☐ Write down the big idea in your journal.

3

WHAT DOES THIS ALL MEAN?

In step one, you begin to learn how to become familiar with observation. You are observing words, context, and even marking paragraphs. If this is your first time through the process, you may stop and think, "What good is it to know where the paragraph is when I don't know what the paragraph means?" Rest assured – you are not alone when you have that feeling. Before we jump into the meat of this book, let's review what we have already accomplished.

In the beginning, you dealt with your motives for Bible study and learned that the ultimate reason for studying the Bible is to know God better. Then, you received some tools that could be trusted to help with basic Bible study. In the last chapter, you learned some principles of observation that will help you do more than simply read a text; it will enable you to study a text. This brings us to the second step in our process.

Step 2: Interpretation

As we come to this section, it's time to learn some basic principles of interpretation. The more you use these tools, the more it will become second nature as you study the Bible. Have you noticed that some people can simply spend a few moments with a text and they already know the Big Idea, the context of a passage, and what the writer's intent was when he wrote to his audience? Is this some special gift given only to preachers? I really don't believe it is. Sure, some people have a theological mind, and others have a practical mind – we can't deny that. Yet, at its core, the reason some can interpret a passage so quickly is very simple: ***they have been doing it a long time!*** What's the difference between an accomplished pianist and a beginner? The answer, over-simplified perhaps, is two fold: *time* and *discipline*.

Think back to when you learned to ride a bike. Did you use training wheels? Do you still have training wheels? (Don't answer that at loud!). Remember learning to drive a car? Were you super-attentive to details, doing a mental checklist (sometimes even a verbal one)? How long have you been driving now? Do you have the radio going, one hand on the wheel, carrying on a conversation with your spouse in the front, eating your food on the go, and watching the kids in the back through the rearview mirror – all at "Godspeed!" How can you do all this? You have been doing it a long time...

Before we start this chapter together, you may picture yourself on "Bible-study training wheels." Perhaps you hear the voice in your head saying, "Remember this…don't forget that…make sure I check here…ask this question now…" Don't get discouraged or even feel overwhelmed. Work through the process again and again and one day you will stop and think, "When did I lose my training wheels?"

You are an investigative reporter

Do you remember the bumbling detective, Columbo? He always asked questions – and that's how he gathered information. He may have appeared foolish to others, but there was a method to his madness. And there's a method to this madness here as well.

If you are studying a passage from the New Testament, you are beginning with a document that was written nearly two thousand years ago. Stop and think about what you just read. Two thousand years ago, John 3.16 was first penned. It was penned in a different part of the world, in a different language, in a different culture, and a different political climate.

There are no living witnesses left for you to interview to help you understand the cryptic message that has been left behind. As an investigative reporter, you sense that there is a story here, but how will you crack the case? Simply stated, an investigator's "go-to" tool is the art of the question. Yet, you are not questioning people; you are questioning the text. What does that look like?

Who wrote it?

This is important because even though the Bible is a divine book, it was penned by human authors. These people had their idiosyncrasies, vocabularies, and tendencies just like people today. As I study the Bible, I will come to understand that Paul and James use a slightly different meaning for the word *justify*. They are not contradicting each other – they are simply telling the truth with their vocabularies. Even though both Mark and Luke write a Gospel account of the life of Jesus, they are vastly different. Luke is much longer than Mark. Why is that? Why does Matthew use the phrase, "That it might be fulfilled" or "as it was written" so many times? These are human elements to the story.

If you enjoy reading, then you can understand that people have favorite authors and ones that they would rather not read. Some writers have a flair for words – others are very bland. Some writers help you visualize what you are reading; others have no imagination at all. To some extent, this is true of the biblical writers as well. Luke, a doctor, had an eye for detail. This characteristic comes through in his writings. Consider that Luke wrote only two books (Luke and Acts), yet, in sheer volume, this represents nearly one quarter of the New Testament!

As you become more familiar with the human elements of each writer, you will notice some habits that are hard to break. Paul generally mentions grace and peace to every one he writes to. Luke is a visual guy who provides as much detail as possible. John rarely uses more than a two-syllable word. Mark, in writing to the Roman world, presented Jesus as one whose greatness was found in how He served – and in how busy He was. Yet, regardless of all the human subtleties, the beauty behind this is that each is conveying God's truth to us accurately.

To whom did he write?

Usually in the first two verses of a New Testament letter, you can find something about the audience. This is more general in the Old Testament as almost every letter is connected to the Jewish people during the time of writing (with a few exceptions as Obadiah addressed Edom; Jonah and Nahum address Nineveh).

Why is this information helpful? Consider the three exceptions listed above from the Minor Prophets. When you see to whom they wrote, your "observation lens" should be out and your investigative curiosity should be asking questions. Who was Edom? As you pull out your encyclopedia or dictionary, you find that Edom is another name for Esau, the brother of Jacob (who was called Israel).

Who were the Ninevites? Nineveh was the capital city of the Assyrian Empire. Well, who were they? The Assyrians carried the Northern Kingdom (Israel) into captivity. These were fierce people – the very mention of their names struck fear into the hearts of seasoned soldiers. When you start to understand something about these people, you can read the background of Jonah…there was a reason he was hesitant to take God's message to these fierce people.

Understanding the audience helps in the New Testament as well. For example, John writes The Revelation to the seven churches in Asia Minor. Before we unpack that, can I share a personal pet peeve that could be avoided with a little observation? This book often is called the Revelation of St. John the Divine, or something similar. Yet, read the opening verses and it is specifically called, "The Revelation of Jesus Christ." (OK, rant is now complete – Thank you!)

Many good people have tried to take some mystical approach to these seven churches. Each church is symbolic of a specific time frame during the Church Age. We are now in the Laodicean Age, and so forth. I'm not trying to be critical – and I grew up hearing this teaching often. Yet, there are some simple problems with this interpretation. Consider:

1. No two people can agree on when one "age" starts and the next begins.

2. This teaching ignores the fact that all seven churches existed at the same time!

3. This teaching only works for American churches! (It would be hard to tell a Chinese or Filipino Christian in the vibrant churches in that part of the world that he is living in the Laodicean age.)

Is there another way to use this information? Yes, but it doesn't preach nearly as well! If we were working through Revelation, then hopefully during our observation stage we would pull out a map and locate these seven churches. If so, here is what we would find. John addresses each church in a sequential order. Why? He is utilizing a postal delivery service. Now, I know different church ages preach better – but I just can't buy that this was John's intent. That meaning will never come "out of the text" itself (exegesis). Only the reader (from a 2,000 year gap) can bring this idea to the text (eisegesis).

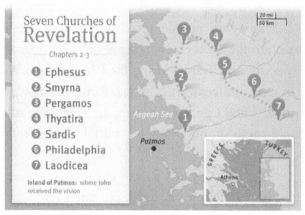

Map of the seven churches Jesus Christ addressed in Revelation 2 and 3 (artwork by Kelly Cunningham)

Why did he write?

Was the apostle addressing a problem? Was he commending and praising a job well done? Why do we have four gospels (Matthew, Mark, Luke, and John)? Why does Matthew use this one phrase repeatedly, "As it was written…" but Mark rarely does? The reason is not mystical – it is found in understanding their audiences. Matthew wrote to a primarily Jewish crowd to show Jesus as their promised king. Mark wrote to a busy Roman crowd who was impressed by acts of service – so, Jesus is portrayed in this light.

John specifically tells us the reason he wrote his gospel in John 20.31. Let me ask you a question: Why is Ruth in the Bible? Did God feel that He should include a romance story for the women who read the Bible? Actually, the purpose for this small book is found in the end of the story. Ruth marries Boaz and they have a son, Obed. He has a son named Jesse. Ruth's great-grandson was a little boy named David. The writer is introducing us to David more than anything else. The introduction of David is helping to carry on the redemptive thread, anticipating a "greater Son of David" who will come in the future.

When did he write?

Sometimes, I am just curious as to what else is going on in the world when an event takes place. When I know the time frame, I then pull out a simple Google search: "What was happening in the world in 1000 BC?"

James wrote his epistle probably between 45-50 AD. He had grown up as the younger brother of Jesus, yet was not a believer until after the Resurrection. Interestingly, while followers of Jesus were writing down His teachings, during this same time, followers of the Buddha were writing down his teachings as well. These two competing "canons" were being developed at roughly the same time, yet in two different regions of the earth.

Where did he write?

In the New Testament letters, it is sometimes helpful to know where Paul was when he wrote back to a church. When you are reading an event, where does that event take place? For example, in the book of Acts, every chapter seems like you have traveled to at least one city. What can you learn about the place to where the book was written? Learning the customs of that city, learning to think like those people – this enables you to understand the message just like those hearers would have understood.

For example, as you read Acts 16, you notice that in Philippi, Paul did not go to a synagogue first (as was his custom). Instead, he met a group of ladies (along with Lydia) by the river. What does this suggest about Philippi? For one, it suggests that it was not heavily populated with Jewish men (or there would have been a synagogue). This city was like a miniature Rome, where his Roman citizenship should have been greatly expected. Little bits of information like this add "color" to an otherwise black-and-white interpretation.

What did he write?

What is the big idea for the book, for the passage? Why did Paul write to people in Philippi? What happened to Paul in Philippi? In Acts 16, he was arrested along with Silas. He had the opportunity to lead the jailor to Christ. Also in this city, Lydia (the seller of purple) and a demon-possessed woman help form the nucleus to a new church.

When he writes back to this church, there is no strong rebuke. He is not dealing with a major problem. Instead, he continually mentions "joy" and "rejoice" throughout the epistle. This repeated theme helps to unlock the big idea for the book.

Basic rules to remember...

Since this is Bible Study 101, we limit our rules to just a small handful. Anything else would just be overwhelming. However, if you master these rules, you will be able to dig much truth out of the Scriptures that sometimes are simply resting beneath the surface – just waiting to be discovered.

The Golden Rule

A man named Cooper gets the credit for coming up with a very common-sense rule. Allow me to paraphrase his rule: If the plain sense makes common sense, then any other sense would be nonsense! What does this mean?

Basically, the good doctor was saying that as you read Scripture, see if the face value of the text makes sense. If it doesn't, then you may be dealing with something poetical, figurative, or metaphorical. But, if the plain, literal sense of the text makes common sense, don't go looking for some hidden meaning.

Here are some examples to test out his rule:

1. Jesus said, "I am the door…"

   The plain literal sense of "door" is that which turns about on hinges and can be locked from the inside. Does common sense compel us to take Jesus' words literally? No – for that would be nonsense. So, in this example we look to find what type of analogy could be made from a door that would describe Jesus. We scour the context of his words and see if His comments (in context) have already been defined.

2. What do you know about the Good Samaritan?

   One of the early church leaders, Origen (who lived in the early 200s), used a less-than-literal approach to this story. Here is what he taught: The man who was robbed is Adam. Jerusalem is paradise and Jericho is the world. The priest is the Law and the Levites were the prophets. The Samaritan is Christ and the inn is the Church. You may be thinking, "I've never seen that before!" – And neither did Jesus! That's the point.

When I read that story, I think, "the inn is an inn; the Samaritan is a Samaritan, the priest is a priest, etc." Why? Because the plain sense just makes common sense. A less than literal approach is nonsense.

The First Mention Rule

This principle is not a hard and fast rule, but it is useful. The general concept behind this thought is that the Bible introduces a concept in its simplest terms in the beginning and then moves into the complexities of the doctrine, word, etc. So, by tracing the first mention of something, we can get a glimpse into how the Bible uses the term.

It is not an infallible rule. Consider that the first time the word *serpent* is used it is in reference to Satan. Yet, in the book of Numbers, Moses lifts a serpent on a pole for the nation's healing. John tells us that that this was a picture of Christ (a polar opposite of the first mention of the word!).

The Comparison Rule

Let the Bible interpret the Bible for you! Sure, there are over forty different *human* authors, but there is only one Divine author standing behind the text. This is where a good study Bible comes in handy. Study Bibles provide these cross-references for you either in the center margin or after each verse. R.A. Torrey has the *Treasury of Scripture Knowledge* with nearly 500,000 cross-references, which might be worth considering as part of your toolbox later (for now, a good study Bible is great for learning how to develop the habit of studying Scripture).

The comparing-scripture-with-scripture method provides more clarity by gathering all the related information on a particular topic. For example, consider Paul's terminology "old man" as used throughout his epistles. You are reading through Romans 6 and come to verse 6:

> *Knowing this, that our **old man** is crucified with him, that the body of sin might be destroyed, that henceforth we should not serve sin.*

I hear people today sometimes talk about "my old man" but I don't think they mean the same thing Paul did.[1] By looking at Colossians 3:9-10 we learn that we "put off" the old man and "put on" the new man. This thought is repeated in Ephesians 4:22-24. There are other verses that *Treasury of Scripture Knowledge* will direct me to, but overall, it appears that Paul is referencing spiritual renewal. There is a conscious decision that we must make to put off one and put on the other. It is not automatic.

---

[1] Old man has a slang connotation today. "I wanted to go with you guys, but my old man wouldn't let me..." Usually it means a father, but can also be used to refer to a boyfriend, spouse or significant other. Obviously (using common sense) this is not what Paul meant!

It doesn't change meaning over time!

Stated succinctly, it cannot mean what it never meant. Earlier you read the *interpretation* of the Good Samaritan by Origen. While some would say about his interpretation, "That'll preach!"[2] – in reality we should note that no one who heard the original parable understood it that way. And if we understand a story differently than when it was originally given, then we are not using exegesis. Instead we are bringing our culture to the text (eisegesis).

To my knowledge, the following anecdote has never happened. It is being provided as an example of what not to do. In this proverbial sermon, the preacher turns to Luke 13:13 and reads,

> *And he laid his hands on her: and immediately she was **made straight,** and glorified God.*

The good reverend then goes on to preach about how God can cure the gay and help him be straight. The problem is simple – in the context, *straight* is the opposite

---

[2] "That'll preach" is a preacher's phrase. It carries the idea that someone has a good thought and people will be excited to hear it.

The point I want to make here is that while some thoughts are exciting to hear – this is not as important as asking the question, "What does this mean?" Often "Remove not the ancient landmarks" will be "preached" in the services today that are not contextually accurate. This passage will be observed momentarily.

of "bowed together" (crooked). This woman had been bent over for 18 years…Jesus made her straight. That's all it means – and it cannot mean what it never meant.

Remove not the ancient landmarks! Now, that will preach! We have the landmark of the Bible, the landmark of holy living, the landmark of separation, and of soulwinning, etc. We can even alliterate this to make it feel more like a sermon outline: The Landmark of Scriptures; the Landmark of Sanctification; the Landmark of Separation; the Landmark of Soulwinning…

However, a *landmark* was a rock that marked the land's boundary. To move someone's landmark was to steal his land and claim it as one's own. So, to preach this verse in context, we would actually be preaching, "Do not steal from your neighbor…" – but that doesn't look nearly as exciting as our [non-textual] sermon we listed!

As Bible interpreters, we need to get used to asking, "How would this audience have understood this letter / book when they received it?" Our task is to understand the passage as the original hearers would have understood it. Whatever was written before us was written for our admonition, for our learning. That which was written will never mean what it has never meant.

Context is always king...

Think of the statement, "That was a ball!" It's only four simple words – and you know what every single word means. Yet, you cannot accurately give the person's meaning without context. Does he mean, "I had a great time...?" Maybe he means, "This was a formal dance that I attended." Maybe he is an umpire at a baseball game. Without a clarifying sentence – a context – the sentence is ambiguous. In like manner, if Scripture is not left within its context, people can make it "mean" whatever they want. That's wrong...and it's dangerous.

Perhaps the most used verse by people who do not attend church is Matthew 7:1, "Judge not that ye be not judged." Immediately, this verse is taken to mean that sinners can do what they please without any fear of judgment. Perhaps the least known verse could be Matthew 7:2! In context, Jesus is not saying, "Don't ever judge another person...just love them!" In fact, He is actually warning them to judge *righteously* and not hypocritically. He is not against judgment – He is against hypocritical judgment. Context makes all the difference.

Without heeding context, the Bible has been used to teach all sorts of weird ideas. Those hostile to the Bible are often guilty of cherry-picking verses from the Old Testament and trying to paint God in a bad light. They refuse to look at context. Among fellow believers, sometimes it is staggering to think about all the vastly different end-times rapture positions Matthew 24 allegedly teaches! How can one passage teach that believers will go through the Tribulation; they will not go through the Tribulation; and that they will go only through the first half of the Tribulation? *Methinks it has something to do with context!*

So, this begs the question: How do you frame something in its proper context? I know we often encourage Bible memorization (and we should) and we claim certain *promise* verses (Praise the Lord for His promises) – but the danger is that we can mistakenly begin to think that each verse is *independent* from the rest.

So, for example, a preacher can preach verse-by-verse and actually teach things that the first recipients of those letters would not have seen (or that the writer did not intend). At the foundational level, the <u>paragraph</u> and not the verse is the basic unit for understanding the Bible. Understanding this, here are some basic reminders for reading the Bible in context:

1. Locate the paragraph(s) for what you are reading (sometimes called the "near context")
2. Look for the main idea (every paragraph has a main topic).
3. Observe the parts of the paragraph and how the writer supports his topic.
4. Ask how your paragraph first within the chapter and the book you are reading (the "larger context").

Setting the Bible in context is neither a spiritual gift nor an innate talent. It is a skill set, much like playing an instrument. If you have the privilege of having a child who plays an instrument that is pleasing to the ears – you may remember that it did not always sound like that! If you have a child who enjoys the piano today, you may also remember the times they simply didn't want to practice…If you preached to them about the need to practice anyway, then be aware there may be days you may have to take your own advice when it comes to Bible study!

What type of literature?

The technical term in this step is recognizing the genre. Is it narrative, poetical, an epistle, prophetic, etc.? Perhaps, its primary purpose is teaching. The genre does give us clues on what to expect. In the poetical sections, I should expect to find figurative language (the Lord is a shield and buckler, a strong tower, and many other images). In narratives, I am looking at the main characters, the plot, and the purpose of its inclusion into the text.

Narrative
A common genre in the Bible is **narrative**. This is basically a story – and we've all heard them. Joshua marched around Jericho. David killed Goliath. Cain killed Abel. Noah built an ark, etc. In the New Testament, Jesus calms a storm or heals someone. Paul preaches in Athens. Peter confronts Ananias and his wife.

While these stories are relating *history*, as Bible readers we cannot forget that they are also related *theology*.

How do we know this? Because "all scripture is given by inspiration of God and is profitable…" Because the "things that were written aforetime were written for our admonition and learning." These historical-theological accounts are selective in nature. The writers did not write *everything* that happened – so in observation we ask, "Why did they choose this event? What is the significance here and what can I learn from it?" There is a reason that this particular story was chosen and not others.

Poetry

Another common genre is **poetry**. Psalms and the Song of Solomon would contain large portions of poetic material. At times, there is a misconception concerning this genre. Poetry in the Bible is not like, "Jack and Jill, went up the hill…" Poetry in the Bible is based less on rhyming words and more on parallel thoughts (one could say, "rhyming thoughts").

Can I share one more pet peeve? It is Psalm 23, not Psalms 23. It is the book of Psalms (plural, because it contains more than one psalm). There, I feel better – thanks for listening.

Wisdom

The Bible also contains **wisdom**. You see this in Job, Proverbs, and Ecclesiastes. James in the New Testament would mirror some of this as well. Wisdom is practical, general principles for life. But be careful to read in context. For example, don't simply pull out a verse from one of Job's friends and assume it's good theology. The friends are rebuked at the end of the book by God. In like manner, Solomon talks about the vanity and emptiness of life – don't assume this is the lot in life for believers because we know that Jesus came to give us abundant life!

Prophecy

Another genre that sometimes can present a daunting task for interpretation is **prophecy**. In the Old Testament, a large percentage of the books were written by prophets – and this is more than simply the "Major and Minor" prophets.

Within prophecy, our tendency is to think of predicting the future – yet, this was not the major thrust of their message. Prophets dealt with both foretelling (about the future) and with forth-telling (about the present). If we don't understand this, and we read their literature as though each verse is a prediction – we will miss their intent.

Apocalyptic

A sub-category of prophecy is that of **apocalyptic**. This is literature that reveals (the meaning of the word *apocalyptic*) what is happening behind the scenes in the spiritual world. Often, the prophet would have a vision or some message brought to him by an angel. This message's *plain sense* wouldn't be *common sense* – so another sense was being intended.

Think about reading the book of Revelation without acknowledging the Bible has symbolism – and you will have a mess on your hands! Though we use the *normal* approach to interpretation, we simply don't treat Revelation in the same manner as we treat the Gospel of John (even though they are written by the same individual!). Yes, we use a *normal* approach to both – but it looks differently for each book. The plain sense makes common sense for most of the Gospel. The plain sense doesn't always make common sense in the book of Revelation.

Epistles

A final genre we come across in our Bible is that of *epistles*. No, the epistles were not the wives of the apostles! Rather, *epistle* is a fancy literary term for a letter. Paul wrote letters to the churches he wanted to help. The epistles "read" differently than the gospels. The epistles are not narratives – they are not telling a story. Instead, they are didactic (a word that deals with teaching) in nature and built upon a logical progression of paragraphs.

These epistles are written to specific churches with specific issues and under specific circumstances. In interpreting these epistles, I recommend you understand the historical setting. Where was this church mentioned in Acts? How did it get started? How long was Paul there before he either left or was run out of town? Why is he writing to them now? Did they send a question to him first? If you can do some investigative work here, it opens up clarity for the letter as a whole.

An Inside-Out Approach

One final tool to utilize when trying to understand the meaning of a passage is the inside-out approach. It has already been alluded to by concept; now it's time to put it into practice. Notice how naturally this process unfolds:

1. Define unclear *words* and understand how they operate in its *verse*.
2. Delineate how that *verse* relates to the entire *paragraph* in which it is located.
3. Distinguish how the *paragraph* relates to its *chapter*.
4. Discover how that *chapter* fits with the overall theme of the *book*.
5. Determine how that *book* corresponds to the message of the *testament* it's in.

Do you see it? We started with one word and worked from there all the way out to the testament in which a book is located.

OK – here's the deal. You cannot learn how to drive a car by reading about it. You need to get some behind-the-wheel experience. Bible study is no different. Because I want to see you succeed in this endeavor, I'm not content to simply "lecture" you on the mechanics…I want to involve you! So we come to some exercises…Call it homework if you need to.

In the following examples, you will utilize some of the tools we have introduced to answer some basic questions about these selected texts.

Example 1: Read 1 Corinthians 13

Read this short chapter and answer these questions:

Questions to ask	Answers you found
Who wrote this? (Where would you go in a New Testament Epistle to normally find the name of the author?)	
To whom was this writer sending the letter?	
Why did he write it? Was he addressing a problem? Was he praising an action? (Hint: You have to go to the "larger context" to answer this…you will not find it by only reading 1 Corinthians 13.)	
When did he write this? Was he writing any other letters at roughly the same time?	

Where was Paul when he wrote this? Is this significant?	
What is the big idea for chapter 13 (and how do you know)?	

Example 2: Revelation 2.7

After reading this passage, take note of the word *paradise*. Using the principle of First Mention, as well as a concordance, answer the following questions:

1. Where is the first mention of this word? _____
2. Is it mentioned any other place? _____
3. How does your answers shed light on Revelation 2.7? _____

Example 3: Romans 3.24

Read this in a paragraph Bible and let's utilize the Inside-Out Approach.

Steps	Outcomes
Identify unfamiliar *words* (Propitiation). What does this mean?	

How does that concept fit into the *verse*?	
How does that verse align with the *paragraph* in which you read it?	
How does that paragraph fit with *chapter 3*?	
How does Romans 3 with within the theme of the book of Romans?	
How does that theme fit with the big picture of the *New Testament*?	

4

SO WHAT?

Coming to this point in the book, you should have taken the time to pull out some of your books to help you study the Bible. You have spent some time observing the text. You even have worked diligently to interpret the meaning of an ancient text. Great…but so what? I mean, what's the big deal in understanding what some dead guy meant when he wrote over 2000 years ago?

Honestly, do you really care that much about Homer's Illiad or Odyssey? How about Hammurabi's Code? If you think I'm jesting – these pieces of literature were written roughly the same time as some of the parts in your Bible.

Why aren't you spending time observing and interpreting these ancient documents? Frankly – and rather bluntly – if you do not come to the final step of Bible study, you have wasted your time. I know…it's a bold statement. Yet, unless you come to this step, then all you have gained is knowledge. *And knowledge puffs up…*

The final step answers the question, "So what?"

Step 3: Application

This final stage of the journey is when the ancient text is bridged to the modern world. The Bible does not cover every single sin. There is no Bible verse that says, "Thou shalt not smoke." Nor should we expect to find it!

However, there are principles – general guidelines for living a life that pleases God – that can provide assistance with answering some of these "gray areas." When we are trying to utilize these ancient principles in today's world, we are subconsciously going through the process of application.

My task in this chapter is to provide you with four action items to help you carry biblical principles with you and use them for your daily life. After all, if all you have is knowledge, but it doesn't affect your living – so what?

Memorization
David taught nearly one thousand years before Christ this simple thought, "Thy word have I hid in my heart that I might not sin against thee." David did not have a smart phone or a tablet. Nor was his "Bible" leather bound with a red-letter edition. Scripture was bulky, not always the most easily portable. So, what was David to do to internalize God's word? He memorized it.

I'm afraid that the digital era is destroying our critical thinking skills, and undermining the importance of memorization. After all, it's easy to justify the "waste of time" memorizing Scripture when it's always within our grasp. And yet...this principle that David taught is still inspired Scripture. The greater "Son of David" also showed us the importance of Bible memory. In the Great Temptation, Jesus quoted Scripture back to Satan at every turn. I know our devices let us take the Word of God with us. Yet, these truths need to dwell richly *within* us. Having a Bible in our hand is good; having it in our heart is better.

Perhaps you are thinking, "I know I should memorize more Bible verses, but there's just so many, I don't know where to start?" When I was younger, I was challenged to memorize chapters or books from the Bible. I'm sure there was some benefit to that – but in reality, how often are you going to quote a book of the Bible for someone? Our goal is to make this action step practical, which leads us to a how-to section for Bible memory.

The easiest way for Bible memory to be practical, based upon the opinions of many, is to memorize based on a topical system. Rather than memorizing John 3, you would memorize verses on the need for salvation, which would include John 3.

In the following illustration, imagine you are using a 3x5 card to help with Bible memory. On the front side is

a date you started memorizing, the reference, and you may
consider placing the topic as well. On the back side, the
actual verse is written out. Throughout the day, you work
through these verses, learning the topics that interest you.

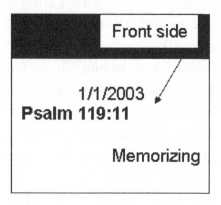

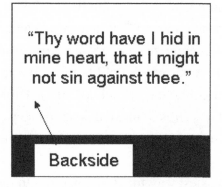

But with which topics should you start? Some
people look for verses to help them with a personal need.
Others have a set of special passages that really minister to
them. There is no right way or wrong way when it comes to
selecting topics. The only caveat is that the verses you
choose to memorize should be properly understood in their
specific contexts. For helpful topic suggestions, check out

the Navigators, an organization founded by Dawson Trotman that was known for their emphasis upon Bible memory and personal application.

Meditation

When Paul was writing to the church at Philippi, a constant theme in his letter was "rejoice." In the final chapter, he provided them some instructions on how to rejoice. His strategy: "…think on these things." The command comes just after Paul's list of things that are lovely, good report, virtuous, etc. To "think on these things" is another way to describe meditation.

Now, we are not talking here about transcendental meditation where you are humming and looking for your inner self. That's not biblical meditation. Meditation in the Bible was illustrative of how a cow ruminates on its food. It takes the food down, then brings it back up to get more nutrients, then sends it back down, then brings it back up, etc. So, at its core, meditation begins with Bible intake. You can't meditate (think about) upon that which is not on your mind.

Meditation also assumes that you did not read your Bible simply to check off a daily list. The goal isn't to simply do a duty. Rather, it implies that you have read your Bible with the intent to understand it, with an eye toward general principles, and with an understanding of how your passage fits in its context. Meditation means that you are contemplating, musing, and thinking deeply about what you have read.

Let me *describe* meditation rather than define it. Have you ever heard a song and days later you can't get it out of your head? As I write this chapter, it is Wednesday morning. I woke up still humming a song I heard in church on Sunday. The song was entitled, "We will remember the works of your hands…" For the last 72 hours, I have hummed parts of that song, went online to listen to it again, and thought about the words and meaning it conveys.

On Sunday, I took the song "in…" For the next several days, I have brought the song back "out" so that I could think about it. In essence, the song has helped me to meditate upon the greatness of God's creation and faithfulness. This is the process we want to see you develop in your Bible study.

Here are some simple tips to help you get started developing this discipline:
1. First, *read* the passage.
2. Secondly, *re-read* the passage.
3. Thirdly, *re-read* the passage! (Repeat steps 1-3 as often as is necessary.)
4. Fourthly, *reflect* upon that which you have read. Try to form the meaning of the text in your own words. Look for the big idea, the take away from the text.

5. Fifthly, *respond* to the text. If there is a call to action in your passage, then heeding that call will help you retain these words throughout the day.

The Bible instructs us that application is personal. These things were written for *our* admonition and learning. The word of God is profitable to reprove me, to teach me, to correct me, and to instruct me. Though the Bible is not written *to* you, it is written *for* you.

Internalization

As you are reading this old, ancient book, there is something different about it as opposed to reading Beowulf in a high school literature class. Why? The Word of God is powerful because it is quick, or alive (Hebrews 4.12). You are reading a living book because it comes from the very breath of God (this is the actual meaning of the word *inspiration*). This means we need to take it personal.

Perhaps you have had the unfortunate event of sitting at a Bible study around a table where everyone in the room is discussing a passage. The question that has been asked is simple: "What does this mean to you?" As we have learned already, that is the wrong question because it "cannot mean what it never meant!"

At a foundational level, the real question is, "What does this mean?" Yet, after going through this process, it is fair to ask, "How does this apply to me in my generation, in my culture, and with my daily life?" This question gets to the heart of internalizing Scripture. Here are a few helpful suggestions to consider:

1. Is there a command in the text?
   If there is a command, then the step of internalization is simple – we need to obey it. To summarize James' instruction, we don't want to simply "hear" the Word. We also want to "do" the Word. Knowing the will of God is insufficient. Doing the will of God is of the utmost importance.

   Let me share a quick caveat - not every command is meant to be taken personal. God *commanded* Abraham to offer his son Isaac as a sacrifice. You shouldn't try this at home!

   Try reading through the list of Leviticus and you may have some questions as well. Why? The simple answer is that this book is not given commands to the general public. It is a book that pertains to the Levites, who are instructing the Israelites, etc. In the Ten Commandments, one specifically says we are to "Remember the Sabbath" – yet Christians worship on Sunday rather than Saturday. Why? Specifically, Exodus 32 tells us that God gave the Sabbath as a sign for Israel – and we are not Israel. This explains why the New Testament repeats nine out of ten of these commandments – but does not enforce Sabbath-keeping upon the church.

2. Is there a general principle in the text?
   If the text contains a principle, I should follow it. In the book of Leviticus there are many commands we don't follow. Yet, those words are still inspired, still profitable, and still written for my learning. So what am I supposed to learn from irrelevant commands? We need to look for why these commands are given and see if there are general principles we can use for today.

   In Leviticus, what is God wanting to accomplish – where are we in redemptive history? Well, for 400 years Israel has been in an Egyptian bondage. Then, the Exodus came and God brought them out. However, even though they are *physically* out of Egypt, *spiritually* a lot of the Egyptian thinking still remains in them. Throughout the book of Leviticus, God is getting "Egypt out of Israel." He wants to mold them into His people, to have them live differently and separately from the other nations. In effect, He is calling them to holiness. This is the principle we can take away – and is one that Peter actually repeats to New Testament believers in his epistle.

3. Is there a general promise in the text?
   Growing up, I was taught the children's song,
   "Every promise in the book is mine. Every
   chapter, every verse, every line. All are
   blessings of His love divine. Every promise in
   the book is mine." It was a great song – a catchy
   tune…I loved it. The only problem with the
   song was that it wasn't biblical! Here's a
   promise: "I will make of thee a great nation…"
   That was God's promise to *Abraham*, not me!

   Yet, the Bible does give promises that hold true
   throughout time. God promises that He will be
   faithful. He promises wisdom to those who ask.
   He promises to never leave us or forsake us. He
   promises to complete His work within us. He
   promises that He will return back to this earth.

   These promises don't contain the formula of
   "if…then." There are no conditions set. These
   general promises aren't written to one specific
   individual in a specific circumstance. Frankly,
   these promises don't really promise us fortune
   or a happy ending; they promise us of God's
   faithfulness to His work in our lives. These are
   the kinds of promises that we are able to take as
   an anchor, a refuge for our souls.

Summarization

You have memorized Scripture so you can meditate upon it. You have meditated upon it so that you can internalize it. Before we walk away from this passage, we should also summarize it. This process helps us to remember the big idea and it also helps us to meditate and internalize with even more clarity from the text.

As you are working through the application process, here are a few questions to help guide you in summarizing a passage:

1. What does this text teach you about God?
2. What general truth did you learn (about yourself, about mankind, about the world, etc)?
3. Did this passage point out any sin that should be forsaken?
4. Since the Bible is a mirror, what did you see about yourself from this passage?

Conclusion

In this chapter, we have observed four keys to help you make the fruit of your Bible study usable. It's not enough to simply uncover the meaning of a text. What will you do with it? (Or, perhaps more importantly, what will the Bible study do to you?!) Memorization is a lost art, yet we should work to regain it. Meditation has been ripped from a biblical context to where we picture someone in Zen Buddhism. Yet, biblical meditation must be restored.

Internalization is that process of identifying timeless truths that transcend culture, language, people groups, and time itself. It searches for general commands, for general principles, and for general promises that translate into actionable items for today.

Let's leave this chapter with a few practice passages. What application(s) could you make personally regarding them?

Psalm 23

OK – it's familiar…maybe too familiar for you to actually think about what it means. Before you go into quote autopilot, let's make a few observations. More than likely, you are not a shepherd and you do not have a flock of sheep. For me, I live in a desert and I haven't seen green pastures for a while! When I think "rod," it doesn't comfort me…when I think "staff," I think of a church staff. Couple all of this together with the time element – David lived 3,000 years ago. It's an understatement to say, "The world has changed a little!"

Our first tendency is to look for the application. That's backwards. First, look for the meaning so that when you make an application, you know it is aligned with the purpose of the text. Take a moment and either physically write out or verbally walk through the following:

1. Step 1: What did you observe? _____

    _____

    _____

    _____

    _____

    _____

    _____

    _____

    _____

2. Step 2: David is writing poetry, using figures of
    speech. What does he mean? What figures of
    speech does he use? _____

    _____

    _____

    _____

    _____

    _____

    _____

    _____

3. Step 3: So what? How does this truth apply to
    you? The following guiding questions should
    help answer this.
    a. Why should Christians memorize this
        passage?

b. What in this passage should you meditate upon? What truth can you take with you to consider at a future time?

c. What should be internalized? Is there a promise? How about a principle? Or, perhaps there is a command?

d. What is your summary of this passage? In your own words, what has the psalmist meant and how can it be applied in your life today?

_____

_____

_____

_____

_____

_____

_____

_____

_____

_____

John 14:1-6

This verse is sometimes read at funerals. Many people find great comfort here. In the first example, we looked at a passage from the poetical genre. In this example, we are in a narrative. In narratives, we find conversations, stories, parables, teachings, etc. Let's set the context for John 14 before we jump into the interpretation.

In John 13, Jesus has had the Last Supper with His disciples. It's called the "Last" Supper because this is the night in which Jesus will be betrayed, tried before the court of the day, and ultimately condemned to death – and He knows all of this before hand! Knowing this, He has washed His disciples feet and told them that one of them will betray Him.

Jesus has prophesied His own death and that Simon Peter will personally deny Him three times before the rooster crows. After this type of conversation, He launches into our text with those in the Upper Room. This discourse, this teaching moment, continues in John's gospel through chapter 16. In chapter 17, Jesus will excuse Himself from the group and go to the Garden of Gethsemane to pray. There, He will be arrested. It is in the middle of all of this that we come to this text.

Stop for just a moment and think about what you just read. We are getting ready to study John 14:1-6, but we have just located it within a context that covers the span of chapters 13-17 – and we did so with one short paragraph. Setting something in its context doesn't mean we have to write pages of background material. It simply means we need to understand what is happening with that original audience. We use a type of "sanctified imagination" and place ourselves in the story. How would we act? What would we be thinking after Jesus told us He was going to die? How would we respond upon hearing that our "rock" (for this is what the name *Peter* means) was going to deny he even knew Christ?

If we wanted to take this a step further and dig a little deeper, we could ask, "What is the ministry of the Holy Spirit at this point in redemptive history?" When we read chapters 14-16, the big focus is on the coming of the Comforter – but at this point, these disciples have not been indwelt by the Spirit.

The Comforter that goes with us daily has not yet been given to these believers. So, the news they have just received (chapter 13) is like a punch in the gut. They have responded to a message that the "Kingdom of Heaven" is *at hand.* They have believed in the Messiah setting up this kingdom on earth. Now, they hear that He is going to die… Can you feel an emotionally poignant moment? It is at this moment Jesus speaks the words of our text.

1. Step 1: Observation. We have made a few observations already – but what else do you see?

_____

_____

_____

_____

_____

_____

_____

_____

2. Step 2: Interpretation. What is the significance
   of the words of Jesus *in this context?* _____

   _____

   _____

   _____

   _____

   _____

   _____

   _____

   _____

3. Step 3: Application. What do we learn about
   God and Jesus here? What truth can I internalize
   here today for me, right now? _____

   _____

   _____

   _____

   _____

   _____

   _____

   _____

   _____

Philippians 4:13

Perhaps you have "claimed this promise" before. *I can do all things through Christ…* What an encouraging verse! Yet, I can't help but wonder if sometimes this verse just might get used out of context?

Picture this: A MLB player is at the plate, two outs and in the bottom of the ninth. It's now a full count. If he strikes out – the game is over. He loses. But, he is a Christian. From his Sunday school days years ago, he remembers this phrase – "I can do all things through Christ who strengthens me…"

His mind goes calm, and the next pitch is sent out over the right field fence. As he is carried off the field, he points to the sky to acknowledge his Savior – what a moment! Question: Was this an accurate application of the verse? If not, why not? If so, why? What is the key to understanding whether or not an application is valid? Context is king.

In the previous examples, we have practiced with poetry and narrative. Now, in this final example from Philippians we have a didactic (teaching) section from an epistle. Let's work through it.

1. Step 1: Observation
    a. What are you seeing in this text?

b. What do you know about this book already, this city, Paul's missionary journey here in the book of Acts, etc?

_____

_____

_____

_____

_____

_____

_____

2. Step 2: Interpretation
   a. What is the near context?
   b. What is the context of this book?
   c. Are there any words that should be defined? (Communicate, vs 14)
   d. How does this verse fit in with its paragraph? (Verses 10-19 are the paragraph)
   e. How does this paragraph fit in with the theme of the book? (Rejoicing)

_____

_____

_____

_____

_____

_____

_____

3. Step 3: Application
    a. Did you notice that Paul is talking about them financially supporting him?
    b. This church was the only church that did. They took care of him again and again (v10, 14, 16).
    c. What specifically was Paul talking about being able to do in this context?
    d. By the way, this exercise will also help you to rightfully apply verse 19 – another verse often taken out of context.

_____

_____

_____

_____

_____

_____

_____

_____

You have just walked through three examples from three different genres. The questions that guided you showed you that we approached each section slightly different – but with always the same goal in mind. We wanted to seek to understand the meaning of the passage so that we could make the application personal.

YOU CAN DO THIS!

We are dealing with three simple steps: Observe, Interpret, and Apply. These three steps are the secret to Bible study. These are the steps you take to endeavor to understand the Bible on your own. You picked this book up because something inside you wants to be more adept at personally understanding the Bible. A book of this size cannot possibly go through every single passage in the Bible. Yet, you are not being left on your own!

Throughout this book, we have worked through different genres, different passages, and worked diligently to understand each sample *in its context*. I have tried to hold your hand and walk you through these steps. If you're a parent, you know what comes next. It's time to encourage the new student to try it personally.

Years ago, I heard how the mother eagle teaches its eaglets how to fly. It sounds like animal cruelty! The eaglet hops on mom's back and nestles in for a comfortable ride, enjoying the wind in its face. The ride is pure enjoyment until… Mom decides to fly upside down causing the eaglet to fall through the air.

The mother squawks encouraging "words" to the eaglet that roughly translates to, "If you don't open your wings and fly, you're gonna die!" The mom then will fly under the eaglet and that eaglet doesn't know what just hit it! It has a death hold on mom and is ready to get back to the nest. Mom, however, has other ideas.

Mom starts the flight back home, only to turn upside down causing a repeat of what just happened. In fact, mom will do this several times until little junior figures out that the "fun" will not end until he flies. Why is mom doing this? The answer is really quite simple: because she really believes that it is vital for the success of her young that they learn to fly. In the truest sense, it is a sink or swim experience.

When it comes to understanding the Bible, it is vital that every believer learns how to personally interpret and apply the Bible as well. As Christians, we cannot live from Sunday to Sunday…we have to hear from God when our pastors aren't around. If this is a new experience, you can relate to the fear of the young eaglet. Yet, I want you to also relate to the fact that there are some people squawking out encouragement to you…You really can do this!

For a while, your study will be very methodical. "Did I observe long enough? Did I ask enough questions? Am I sure this is what the passage means? Am I applying this correctly?" But these questions reflect the "training wheels" stage – it doesn't last forever. The more you practice, the more this becomes second nature. So go ahead – go for it.

In this final section, I want to point you in the right direction with some practical suggestions on where to begin. You know you need to observe, interpret, and apply. You have your tools ready to launch. Yet, perhaps you still have this nagging question, "Where do I begin?" Consider the following suggestions:

1. The parables Jesus told
2. A topical Bible study on the love of God
3. A narrative from John's gospel (Jesus deals more with the individual in John's gospel and more with the crowds in Matthew, Mark, and Luke)
4. Portions of Mark's gospel (no fluff, right to the point)
5. Philippians (though chapter 2:1-11 will be a theologically rich section)

I also wanted to offer some suggestions on where NOT to start as well:

1. Leviticus
2. Hebrews
3. Galatians
4. Revelation
5. The Old Testament

The last suggestion will encourage some and surprise others. Why would I not simply challenge you to start at Genesis and work your way through the Bible? As Jesus said in John 5, the entire thrust of the Old Testament points to Christ. By starting with the New Testament, we can become familiar with the overall theme of where Scripture directs. Granted, this is a little bit of a catch-22 as well. In reading the New Testament, the writers assumed that their audience had a grasp on the Old Testament contents. So, what are we to do? Should we just simply read the Bible for a few years before we ever start to study it? I don't believe that's practical – nor do I believe that is the heart of God. Therefore, I suggest starting with the New Testament, and then slowly working through some of the Old Testament texts as you become familiar with the three-step process.

Thank you for downloading this book! I appreciate your feedback, and I love hearing what you have to say. If this book has helped you, let me know. Your feedback will help any revisions become even better. Send me an email at mike@jmichaellester.com with questions or comments.

I'd greatly appreciate it as well if this book was helpful if you'd leave a positive review on Amazon.

Many thanks!
Mike

Are you interested in writing a book?

If you feel like writing a book is an overwhelming task, it's not as difficult as it seems. The staff at Self-Publishing School helped me – and they can help you as well with their FREE VIDEO SERIES to help you get published in *just three months*.

Are you busy? No problem! Not the greatest writer? That's ok! Not even sure where to start? Maybe a little bit afraid of the whole process? Fine – these people walk you through it step-by-step. They are the <u>only</u> resource you need from start to finish to help get you published.

Want more information?

https://xe172.isrefer.com/go/sps4fta-vts/bookbrosinc4019

You're Welcome!

About the author

I grew up in a pastor's home in the state of Georgia. The Bible has always been a part of my life. My granddad was a pastor, great-granddad as well – also many of my uncles have been in ministry as well. I went to Bible college in Tennessee and that's where I met the love of my life, Jen. We were married in 1995 and shortly after we moved to California to serve with Lancaster Baptist Church and West Coast Baptist College. Our family has grown – today we have five daughters and our oldest is now in college sitting in my classroom.

In ministry, I serve as the academic dean of West Coast Baptist College and one of the singles' pastors at Lancaster Baptist Church. My heart's desire is to see people not only read the Bible, but also understand it. Sometimes I say it this way: "Learn the Book; Love the Book; Live the Book! I hope this book has helped me to accomplish that goal and that you now have a greater desire to study God's Word.

Made in United States
North Haven, CT
15 August 2023

40332204R00061